George,

WHAT CAN I SAY!?

Holy CRAP

This is GOING TO BE FUN

So GLAD TO BE ABLE TO WORK WITH YOU.

Sam Aug 9/14

THE
SUSTAINABLE
STARTUP

*(Building the right team for
the right project.)*

CAMERON CHELL & JAMIE CLARKE

CONTENTS

In memory and honour of my Father,
Arthur Lionel Chell

FOREWORD

by Arden Styles
COO of Business Instincts Group

Your startup will probably fail.

Sure, some are wildly successful, and with it they bring strato-
spheric valuations. But the fact remains most startups will fail.

What makes the difference? What is the magic mix of people,
process, and strategy that work together to increase the chance
that a startup becomes a thriving and sustainable business?

Years ago I met an entrepreneur who had those answers. A
twinkle in his eye, a leather jacket on his back, and a singular
focus on success, all defined his persona. With swift confi-
dence he was able to apply a special alchemy to his startups: a
combination of bold vision, ruthless determination for success,
and a healthy dose of luck. Yes many of his startups failed.
But - several succeeded and have become the stuff of legend.
And what a learning experience it was.

Still, could it be that there are too many startups and not enough
businesses? The road to startup failure is paved with good
ideas, best intentions, and passionate people. The hardest
part is crossing the chasms from startup to sustainable market
offering, to long-term successful business. Entrepreneurs need
to realize that a good idea is not enough to create a sustainable
startup. Those seeking to commercialize a product or service
need to think beyond the idea itself and consider all elements
necessary for a strong business. After all, the success of a
startup is only measured by its sustained ability to deliver value

into the marketplace. At this point it is no longer a startup, but a viable business.

Throughout my career I have had the privilege of working with businesses of all shapes and sizes, across many different industries. I have seen what works, and what doesn't. In many of my assignments I confidently applied theories, methodologies, and approaches espoused to me while in business school. While these approaches had their purpose, there always seemed to be a missing X-factor to increase the chance of success. A key question for me during my career has been - do the theories and approaches reflect the reality of the business world?

The reality of the business world is that entrepreneurs are rewarded for creating, not competing. No amount of methodology or theory can replace the basic need to create. Creating something new and making something better is at the heart of the entrepreneurial spirit. The entrepreneur I met all those years ago was able to take an abstract idea and create real value in the marketplace. Each of his startups begins with the most powerful question of all - why? Answer the why, in a way that no one has before, and your startup has a good chance of becoming sustainable on its way to becoming a thriving business.

The entrepreneur I refer to is Cameron Chell. A serial entrepreneur whose vision, experience, and insight drive success for his team, the businesses they create, and the communities where they live.

Now Cameron, along with Jamie Clarke, a Senior Analyst with Business Instincts Group, have captured his proven ideas and principles in this book. In it, they describe their seven principles for creating sustainable startups so that they can become successful businesses. By applying these principles to their startups, entrepreneurs can leverage the ideas and insights of someone who has been there before.

Not once.

Not twice.

But many times.

Creating a startup takes guts. Developing a sustainable startup takes smart execution.

Read this book, apply the principles, and help create something new that leaves a lasting impact on the marketplace.

Good luck on the journey. It is fraught with unknowns and hidden challenges. But in the end, it will be worth it.

INTRODUCTION

Welcome to the Sustainable Startup.
The methodology behind creating a Sustainable Startup is rooted deeply in real world experience. Doing away with hypothetical circumstances, or managerial tests, and focusing on the real situations startups find themselves in allows one to incorporate their experiences and grow from them.

What most startup methodologies focus on is creating the perfect cycle of ideation, creation and iteration. It is a system that is well established and has been discussed at length, thus it is imperative that startups understand these cycles because they are the integral parts to proper scaling. More often than not, however, they do not focus on the people that form the startup teams. Both teams and the right product fit are essential for creating a startup that lasts, but when the going gets tough, it's the team that puts the company on their back and gets it back on track.

The Seven Principles that will be outlined throughout the book are based on Three Principles themselves.

The first is the knowledge that Sustainable Startups are counterintuitive. Most books on leadership will focus on how you will achieve certain goals, how you will be the best in your industry and how you will sell the most products. In a Sustainable Startup you realize that when you establish why your startup exists, your how will be constantly evolving.

Secondly, most works on creating a startup, or running a successful business, will focus on finding the ideal leader. In a Sustainable Startup you will realize there is no such thing as the right or the ideal leader; there are only leaders that help their teams and startups to excel. Along these same lines, a Sustainable Startup focuses on principles and not rules. Rules force companies along certain paths with terms like "3 Ways To..." or "How To..." where as principles seek to guide and supply methods for growth.

The third principle that Sustainable Startup operates upon is the knowledge that this is not the definitive work on startups. Instead this is part of a community and movement that promotes guidelines and methodologies to create strong long lasting startups. Works like the 4 Steps to the Epiphany or Lean Startup are complimentary publications that operate in conjunction with comparable thoughts and methodologies to Sustainable Startup.

Building a Sustainable Startup means entrepreneurs understand that the path to success will not always be a smooth journey. It's about finding the right team that will put the startup on their back to carry it across the chasm between failure and success.

- Cameron Chell

Entrepreneurs, by their very nature, want to create. They work and work on a project and see it through to completion before moving on to the next one, or they stick with a passion project their entire lives, but creation is in their DNA. While many entrepreneurs are well versed in how to start up a company and what to do with it once it become successful, hurdles are inevitable along the way.

Startups always encounter the chasm, that gap where everything starts to tumble downhill. Bills fall behind, customer attrition begins to take its toll and doubt begins to seep into the daily operations of employees, and founders alike, as to whether or not the lights will be on tomorrow. It's a dark period for startups to operate in and one that a lot have difficulty escaping from. You either escape or enter the deadpool, there's no two ways about it. With Sustainable Startup, our goal is to provide steps for founders and employees to assemble the right team most suited to help carry the startup across the chasm and beyond.

Sustainable Startup is about the team. We step away from focusing on the idea and instead focus on the people. While many startup books focus on what needs to be done as a leader, or how to properly develop a product, we instead realized the benefits of finding and developing the right team for a startup. Hurdles are encountered on a daily basis, and more often than not, a startup's perseverance is a result of the team's efforts, not just the ideas.

In the end it's always about the team, and about the people.

- Jamie Clarke

PRINCIPLE ONE:

STARTUPS CREATE NOT COMPETE

"You can't suppress creativity and you can't suppress innovation."

—James Daly

Creating a successful startup is tricky business. For one, it's never as easy as you think it's going to be, ever. It will always keep you up at night and it will always be on your mind causing a slight source of constant panic. For entrepreneurs, these are good signs. It's the sign you are on the right path. If your startup is not challenging you on a daily basis, it is not the right project. The stress, anxiety and pervasive thoughts that many associate with being negatives are in fact the driving force behind a lot of entrepreneurial genius.

There are, however, two very different schools of thought when it comes to determining the driving force of a startup: Creation and Competition.

Not to say that one method of focus is better than another, as each serves their own purpose, but for a true Sustainable

Startup the focus is placed on creation. There is no denying that startups exist as small players in big markets. It is important to realize that no startup can survive by simply doing one or the other and it is always a matter of finding balance between the two. What we've found is that startups that split their time 80/20 between creation and competition tend to be the most sustainable. The way that these startups often get attention is by whittling away market share or finding new niches they can build off of and creating their own submarkets to own. What this does is expand the marketplace as a whole and creates a larger pie for everyone to take part in, versus digging away at the pie as it already exists. All companies have the goal to find and own a significant portion of whatever market they are playing in, but what distinguishes a Sustainable Startup from a startup focused on competition is their inherent drive to create.

Success, for a competition based company, is built around getting the largest portion of pie possible. With this focus, companies are innovating and creating only a means to stay on pace with others that are trying to take away their market share. Competition based companies take on a very Machiavellian viewpoint of business, thinking that life becomes "us versus them" and each innovation is simply a method to stay ahead of their competition, not to innovate for the sake of improving their product or service offering.

For a Sustainable Startup, success is built around taking a small piece of the pie and growing it exponentially. The focus for these startups is centred on creating and by continually reaching out to their customers, or users, and building what best serves the marketplace. By serving customers and meeting their needs, creation based Sustainable Startups are able to grow their businesses and become more successful. Meeting your customer base where they are and providing them with what they need or want from a product line not only immediately determines the viability of your startup, but shifts the focus of your startup toward a growth orientation.

When a startup focuses on growth and creation they align themselves to serving two needs: reach as many people as possible and create something of use for those people. They aren't concerned with the proverbial selling glasses to the blind, but instead they are interested in being in service to their customer base. The difference between competing and growing are substantial, and often divisive, and only one is the base of a Sustainable Startup. Focusing on daily competition can create success, but it is short lived and therefore in the long run is inconsequential and not sustainable for a business.

STEP ONE: DETERMINING FOCUS

"Be dramatically willing to focus on the customer at all costs, even at the cost of obsoleting your own stuff."

— Scott Cook

Businesses are challenged everyday by the need to keep themselves, and their employees, focused. This is an standard fact that startups must deal with. While it is incredibly important in determining how a startup interacts and encourages its employees, as a whole the company must look at itself and determine what it will choose to focus on.

From here they must establish whether they are going to create or compete on this focus point. Ultimately, these choices will dictate the growth and style that the startup takes on. They are not definitive choices, but they do form a guideline that sets the direction for the company's movement. What is important to remember when determining the focus of a startup is that they define "market dominance" by creating an unfair advantage.

Now this doesn't mean unfair in an unethical sense, far from it. They want to create an advantage that gives them a gain that their competitors cannot easily overcome. In other words, a self-made barrier to entry. Startups do this not just by focusing on creation, but by simply being a better competitor. Working with customers, solving real pain points, validating customer feedback or a product hypothesis, are all methods of creating an organic barrier to entry.

 When a startup is determining their focus the number one goal is to examine their competitors. Marketplaces always have competitors, even down to the tiniest niche; there is someone that is entering into or already established in that space. As a startup, know what distinguishes it from others in the market-place and compile these differences into a list.

The more competitors a startup is able to compile, the stron-ger their understanding will be of their marketplace. Startups that create are able to look at this list, understand where the differentiation points are and find out how to solve recognized pain points.

One of the significant differences between startups that create and those that compete is how they look at this compiled list. Startups that create examine the list of competitors and their offerings and see what they provide, or can give as benefits, above and beyond current offerings. Competitors view this and determine which features they offer that outweigh those offered by the opposition.

Examining features often ends up in the same place. The company does X faster than someone else, or have fees Y times smaller. These aren't massive differentiators, just small differences that can be solved easily by their competitors. Companies that create tend to focus on driving different benefits. A company that is focused on creation tends to be the type to aim for a 40% increase in customer sales or a 25% increase in lead generation. Focus is centred around finding your differentiator and using it to supply benefits to your customer base.

STEP TWO: ENSURING YOU'RE IN BENEFIT MODE

"Every adversity, every failure, every heartache carries with it the seed of an equal or greater benefit."

—Napoleon Hill

There are steps startups can take to ensure they are on the path towards creation. Sustainable Startups are those that are obsessed with their focus. For all intents and purposes, we suggest that these startups are in "Benefit Mode."

Their concern lies with their customers. On a daily basis they are asking what benefit can they provide to their customers? What pain point do they have and what feedback have they given us? This is one of the genuine tests of a Sustainable Startup. The more qualitative data that can be gathered from a customer, the better off the product development cycle for the startup will be. It is important to note that for Sustainable Startups to really grow they need to remain focused on the 80-20 rule, meaning that 80% of the time they must be in "Benefit Mode," while the other 20% should be centred on competition.

This mentality means there must be a lot of interactions with your initial customer base. There are two key questions that Sustainable Startups need to ask their customer base that helps to ensure they are in "Benefit Mode."

What Benefit Do Customers Want?

The more time Sustainable Startups spend with their customers, the more they are able to determine what it is exactly that draws customers in. As a startup is able to acquire this information, getting feedback and notes for iterations, they are able to plot out potential areas of growth. Having this knowledge can help Sustainable Startups build a roadmap of where their growth will take them.

What Will It Take To Implement Customer Wants?

Not that every want or desire will get implemented, but the benefits that customers have laid out as their wants will typically get the highest priority from a Sustainable Startup. During the early stages of a company, it is incredibly important to determine what implementations will be feasible and what the projected growth is. It is tremendously important to note that this feedback from customers is typically the first time a startup steps outside of their vacuum, as it is time for them to validate their hypotheses about their customers.

PRINCIPLE SUMMARY

Principle One is entirely about determining whether or not your Sustainable Startup is going to be one centred on creating or competing. While each are necessary for the other to be successful, typically one consumes the majority of a startup's time.

Startups that tend to lean more toward environments of creation, and generating added benefits for their customers, tend to fit the Sustainable Startup model better than others.

By following Steps 1 and 2, startups are able to make sure they are keeping themselves in "Benefit Mode" and focusing in on customers. By doing so, Sustainable Startups are able to build products that their customers have expressed an interest in seeing and solve their initial pain points. This helps get startups off the ground, to move and grow beyond the walls of their operational vacuums and allows them to begin concentrating on creating a team that is equally focused on creation as they are.

Principle One is about making sure Sustainable Startups are acting in service to their customers, not simply contending against competitors for market share. The difference between the two is monumental.

PRINCIPLE TWO:
YOUR IDEA IS NOT THAT RELEVANT

"In the past a leader was a boss. Today's leaders must be partners with their people... they no longer can lead solely based on positional power."

— Ken Blanchard

Baseball analogies are one thing that runs rampant in the startup world. From hitting singles, to home runs, the analogies of the great American pastime easily convey the message. Following that tradition, there is a lesson to learn and understand about startups the moment you step up to the plate.

YOUR IDEA IS NOT THAT RELEVANT.

Ideas are, simply put, a commodity. As a colleague of ours says, "There is no such thing as an original idea, only original perspective," and people provide that perspective. People are unique and as it relates to the ever changing and immensely competitive environment of startups, the right people are precious. In a world of rapidly changing technology, perspective is what generates originality and without it you just have an idea. In todays world, that idea has been thought of by a hundred people at the same moment as you. It's the people around you and the perspectives they bring to ideas that generate disruptive companies and Sustainable Startups.

If this is the case, then Sustainable Startups are all about the team you collect around you. More importantly, Sustainable Startups are about the team you collect that helps you bridge the gap, fight through downtimes and push to success.

The team you gather must not only have the mindset of an entrepreneur, but they have to be willing to adapt to change at the drop of a hat, quickly grasp new concepts and product iterations and you, as a leader, must exemplify these same qualities. A leader is a teacher, not by holding hands, but by living the qualities you demand of your startup team. As a leader you have to not only be open and willing to be a part of your own exercises, but show the care and patience necessary when teaching and facilitating the growth of others. It takes time, which are three words most startups and their founders hate hearing, but you will notice the valuable difference in hiring the person with the right experience versus hiring the right person for the job.

How do you make your startup sustainable by making it about the people?
The important thing to understand is that these Principles work best when not in a vacuum. Every Principle and every step involved is designed to work in conjunction with every other Principle. We start off our Principles with the one that we believe, if isolated, will give your startup the greatest chance for

success. There are three steps to this first Principle and we'll start by addressing the first step of our first Principle.

The three steps designed to make Principle One work effectively are:

1) Vision
2) Values
3) Alignment

As we continue, we'll be providing you with the step by step processes to make these Principles inherent to your corporate culture. The general mentality in a lot of startup circles is that without a game changing idea your startup doesn't have a chance of success. More often than not, the buzzwords like "Game Changing" or "World Class" are used to hype up a product beyond what it is actually capable of delivering. Realistically, the first thing most people look at when they evaluate a startup is the team that has been assembled and there is a very simple reason for that. Teams ultimately define a Sustainable Startup as they are critical players in its success or failure.

STEP ONE: VISION

"Vision without action is a dream. Action without vision is simply passing the time. Action with Vision is making a positive difference."

— Joel Barker

The most effective way we've come across, in our experiences, to determining the vision of your startup is to find out your Why. Your Why will effectively determine the three key components of your vision: Purpose, Meaning and Cause. Knowing your Why and effectively communicating it, however, are two different things.

In order for your vision to be successful it needs to be clearly communicated to your team. By establishing this clarity amongst your team, you're enabling them to see the full vision of the startup. It is not feasible for everyone to be a rockstar, especially depending on the market you're in, but everyone can be bought in to the vision of your startup. If they aren't striving for the same overarching goals as you, there is going to be some friction down the road. To avoid that, you must communicate to create clarity. To do so, however, there are three questions we use to bring clarity to our vision.

Answering these three questions will determine your Purpose, Meaning and Cause and with those answers you will have your Why. With that in place, you will see why the idea, no matter how great it is, is not the most relevant factor.

1. Why does your startup exist?
When it comes to entrepreneurs, their startup is their baby. It is the reason you get up in the morning. It may also be the reason you never sleep or routinely wake up in a panic in the middle of the night. For the entrepreneur, finding that tenacity comes naturally, but sharing and communicating that passion tends to be a little more difficult. Individuals that are driven to work in startups tend to buy in to lofty ambitions a little easier than their corporately structured counterparts, but that doesn't mean they won't need help understanding your vision and goals.

First and foremost, you need to know why you're startup functions, what it is going to accomplish, and why it is going to do that. Asked another way, what problem does your startup exist to solve? If you can answer that and truly understand what it is solving then you can begin to communicate your idea. Your vision may be of the world changing magnitude, or simply increasing the ease of which users can access a cloud stored file. Either way, if it is solving a pain point your vision will be easy to communicate. Only once you have that established can you move forward to your team and begin to communicate your vision.

2. What difference does your startup make in the world?

While the question seems monumental and potentially difficult to answer, it doesn't have to be earth shattering. The question isn't about revolutionizing the economies of developing countries or curing starvation (though both are highly noble goals), but understanding what your startup accomplishes. No matter what your startup does it is making a difference and in order for clarity to exist that difference has to be recognized and communicated.

While your vision may be to revolutionize private space travel, and that may be the end goal of your startup company, the difference it makes in the world doesn't have to match. If this is the case, the difference your startup creates could be a competitive private space flight market that hasn't existed previously throughout history.

If you don't understand the differences your company is going to make, you're going to have a tough time trying to communicate it to anyone else. From grandiose to simple and overlooked, knowing what you do and communicating what you do are incredibly important facets of a startups growth.

3. Against what (not who) does the startup compete?

When it comes to your competition, it's important to focus on what you're competing against. You should always know who your competitors are in an industry sense, but for a sustainable startup it's crucial to know what you're competing against. Are you competing against shrinking foreign markets or maybe against new legislation that prohibits the importing of a valuable component in production? While it's important to know that Company A is also making a Widget and doing so at $0.30 a product, outside company influences can make or break a startup. If you aren't aware of outside economic factors, knowing the competitor down the street won't save your business.

Once you get your Why you can easily separate yourself from your idea and find that team, that essential group of people that speak to your vision.

Knowing why your startup exists, what it accomplishes and effectively communicating that to your team are two very separate things. Bridging that gap between understanding and communication is what provides both you and your team with the clarity you need to make your startup sustainable.

STEP TWO: VALUES

"Set your expectations high; find men and women whose integrity and values you respect; get their agreement on a course of action; and give them your ultimate trust."

— John F. Akers

If your vision is effectively your Why, values form the compass by which you will be following your vision. Specifically, the values that must be established in a startup company are behavioural values as opposed to core or universal values.

A core value, such as compassion or honesty, or values that are accepted as social norms, are considered to be "table stakes" in the startup environment. These are the bare minimum that leaders and team members should posses. Without core values, those that shape how your startup will grow and the culture it will develop, your startup will be struggling to understand who the right people are. Behavioural values on the other hand fall more closely in line with character traits or specifically designed characteristics. This is not to say that a core value cannot be held as a startups value, more that if you add a characteristic to these pre-existing values they become more explicit and in tune with your organization.

Startups are often viewed as more open and socially flexible than larger corporations. While they may not all be the dress down, show up in a sweatshirt and shorts organizations that the media may depict, the open culture of a lot of startups lends credence to the assumption that they are able to have increased flexibility with their values.

An example of this is taking honesty as one of the core values that you expose in your startup. If you add a characteristic to this such as 'brutal honesty' it becomes more identifiable and specific to your organization. This way of characterizing your values creates the behavioural trends for your startup organization. This isn't to say that 'brutal honesty' becomes the sole mandate that your company operates on, but it does become a tenet by which the company internally operates under.

All of this isn't to say that there aren't other methods or that this will be the correct one for you. There is a plethora of ways to determine what works best for your startup, after all each startup is a different beast than the next. Assigning behavioural characteristics to your values was simply the method we used and have found to be very effective in determining our values and culture.

Want to see how this works in action? Take your team through the following exercise that we use, and have used, to determine what our behavioural values are.

Ask each team member to think of the person they have worked with, read about or know of that they have the deepest sense of admiration for. Allow them to sit and form a picture of this person in their mind. Now ask them to write down the top three personality traits they associate with this person. From here, create a list that consists of all the personality traits mentioned. These become the physical representations of where you and your team can find admiration and respect in others and yourself.

At this point, with your composed list of desired traits, engage your team in a debate as to what your startups top three should be. Note that this should be a very intense and heated discussion with everyone contributing and pushing back to support their ideas. A values brainstorm isn't about offending people, or forcing them to justify their admiration for an individual, rather it is supposed to help create a spectrum of where the employees pull inspiration from and what tenets matter most to them.

During this brainstorming session really push to have your team members not defend solely their own values and ideas, but to view the other suggestions with the same level of respect as they would their own.

In our experience, with more than three values you begin to dilute the culture you are trying to create. By limiting your choice to only three values, you are not saying that others are not important or irrelevant to your startup, simply that the three you have selected are non-negotiable and form the core of your existence. Not selecting core tenets has the same effect as selecting too many. It creates a system too thin to operate under or a system to broad to fully understand. When this is the case it dilutes the importance of creating a strong and unified corporate culture.

STEP THREE: ALIGNMENT

"There can be no happiness if the things we believe in are different than the things we do."

— Freya Stark

Creating alignment is something every business should be doing on a consistent basis. We've talked about how when push comes to shove it's not your idea that's relevant, but your people, and this alignment is what ties that thought together.
People want to belong. If there is only one statement that is universally true it's that one. Humans are social beings and we want to feel that there is a unity with the person beside us. Without that unity we don't feel safe or protected. Professional settings are social gatherings where the people want to fit into an organization and more importantly they want the ability to describe what they do and how that makes a difference in their world.

Inclusion is an immensely motivating factor, but there is more to just being included than people seem to realize. More often than not, people will entertain the idea of letting others into the circle, but nothing beyond that. The key to inclusion is allowing those inside the circle to contribute, as this is the key motivating factor for people. Not only do they want to be included in a company or project, but they strive for ways to contribute something meaningful. Without this, people easily and quickly grow disillusioned. There is always a desire not just to be seen on a level playing field, but to be welcomed as well. Hierarchies always develop in a professional setting and it is almost impossible to avoid, regardless of effort, but while this may be true it doesn't mean that hierarchy should be exclusive. In startup environments where inclusion is bred amongst the founding team, more often than not the hierarchies that form are respected and open. In other words, the CEO or Founders are still approachable and willing to listening to feedback despite their place in the hierarchy.

Creating alignment has always been, and always will be, a nonstop process. There is no master key to open the lock and there is no switch that is guaranteed to turn on that light bulb above your head. There is only an ongoing effort and constant work that must take place and this is what makes a startup so stressful as well as exhilarating. In order to survive, they are in a constant state of creation.

One method we use at Business Instincts Group is to deliver our Personal Elevator Pitch (PEP) in our morning check-ins. Not only that, but each team member delivers their priority for the day and what is going on for them in their personal lives. This allows every member of the team to know and understand what others are doing for the day even if it has no affect on their work day. In a small startup culture, this type of interaction is imperative for helping people inject themselves into their work and to not just feel included, but also understand where they and others fit into the picture.

While the check-in is important for aligning your team with each other, the PEP is critical for aligning each team member individually. Changing or leaving an employee's alignment vague creates an affect similar to a fear of mortality. When an employee is unsure about where they fit in their focus wanders. These employees spend a little longer on breaks, arrive at the office a little later and generally are not as efficient. While it creates this fear of mortality in the employee, it also generates a sever disengagement. Employees become distant, unmotivated and shy away from intuitively approaching projects.

This isn't to take away from the employee's contributions, or the employee as a whole, it is just a general fact that without focus team members are less efficient. Employees, especially in startups, are used to being given a general direction and told to go. In any startup, this direction also involves wearing multiple hats and getting sidetracked. No matter how amazing the employee is it is bound to happen, so keeping an employee aligned and focused helps to minimize this and keep teams on track. Since altering alignment, or lack of individual align- ment, can be so dangerous, it is one of the primary reasons why we focus on the importance of creating alignment within each team member.

The creation formula for your PEP is fairly straightforward:

x+(y1)(y2)=z
The formula, however, isn't the strongest point, but rather is strengthened by the individual elements of the formula and how they create the end result.

X = Your greatest resource.

We like to use a strengths finder to help determine what our top five strengths are as individuals. By no means do you need to use this to discover your strengths, however, we use this resource to give us an unclouded perspective. This helps to determine what resource it is that we must have to complete our job and use the most on a daily basis. Your answers may vary and will most certainly evolve, which will also help to develop your PEP as you grow as a team and as an individual.

Y1 = What you do.

Quite literally this is what you do. Sit by yourself and think clearly about what you spend the most time doing during the work day. What is that one word, or those few words, that define what it is that you do?

Y2 = Who you do it with.
Once you have your **(y1)** clearly defined, ask yourself who you do it with. Who do you spend most of your time working with, training, selling to or raising money from? Your **(y2)** always works in conjunction with your **(y1)**.

Z =What is your result.

This is always going to be the result of your efforts. That's why formulating your **PEP** is always an equation. Your **(z)** is always the result you achieve from your **(x)**, **(y1)** and **(y2)**. As a result, once again sit and think for however long it takes and determine what it is that your efforts result in at the end of the day.

What you will invariably come up with at the end of this procedure is your own **PEP**, your own method to keep yourself aligned on a daily basis. As an example, we'll share Cameron's **PEP** with Business Instincts Group:

I use my **(x)** insight and experience to **(y1)** work with **(y2)** management and investors to **(z)** determine what is most important and specifically how to get it done.

When it comes down to it, and hopefully these three steps have helped to outline this for you and your startup, the idea you have is just not that relevant. At the end of the day, it is the people in your organization that matter. Even in free-flowing work environments, the more structure that an employee has around their role, the more stable they will be. This isn't to take away from the autonomy an employee may have. Time to have ownership on a project is a tremendous growth opportunity for employees, but even autonomous employees need focus and direction. If you can build stability into an employee's career it permits them to experience an open and creative environment. The idea won't make you successful, the people will.

PRINCIPLE SUMMARY

Principle Two of a Sustainable Startup is about creating alignment between the vision and values of your startup. The first step toward doing this is understanding the difference between focusing on the idea and focusing on your people. It's a notion that we stress quite a bit throughout the book because of its sheer importance. Teams of people who can help carry the startup across the chasm when it is needed build sustainable startups. To ensure that this happens, the team needs to have clarity and alignment around the company's core values and vision.

Holding on to an idea and how you are going to accomplish something is a deeply rooted part of being an entrepreneur. Often passion is misplaced and misdirected towards accomplishing a startups 'how' as opposed to their 'why'. In a Sustainable Startup the idea is trivial, it's the people that matter.

Making your Sustainable Startup about the people means taking the time to discover your core values, what the vision for your startup is and how to create alignment amongst your team members, so that you are all working towards the same goals. Ideas are a thing of the past and fundamentally engrained in our image of an entrepreneur. We all want to be the individual, or group of people, that develops a new technology that revolutionizes the world in a monumental way. The problem is that focusing purely on that idea shuts down the ability to see all the pivots and changes that have to happen in a successful startup. When you focus on the individuals that constitute your startup team and loosen the grip on the idea, startups prosper.

PRINCIPLE THREE:

IT TAKES A TEAM TO BUILD A STARTUP

"The goal is not to bend or change ourselves so we fit the norm; the goal is to find the group in which we are the norm. No matter who we are, no matter what our values or beliefs, our tastes or proclivities, there is an entire culture or subculture out there just like us."

— Simon Sinek

When you look at a lot of different management writing that exists, be it books or blogs, there is a strict focus on what we like to think are pretty basic tenets. You'll see a lot of information on alignment, communication, values and vision, because these are the basic things that need to be tacitly understood by a group of people, or in other words, your team. While we believe these are integral parts of any startup, as we laid out in Principle Two, we think the drill-down has to be significantly deeper. Not that these values aren't important, it is just that they lay down the significant foundation that allows Principle Three to carry with it a monumental impact.

A team isn't about finding common ground amongst a group of people, but rather standing on common ground to begin with and using the unique qualities of the individuals to their full potential. Finding common ground should never be the focus of a startup team. If that ground can't be established imme-diately then your startup is already off on the wrong foot. Not only should common ground be instant, it should also be built constantly. It's a delicate balancing act that equates to about 10 people standing on a beam at the same time. Every single person on the team needs to be putting in the same effort as the rest, otherwise you all tip. When teams are aligned they inher-ently know they are working towards something together. There are no misplaced feelings of "I'm doing more work than X," or "X isn't as committed as I am." Team members are able to see exactly how their roles work together and how they influence not only their teammates, but the startup as a whole.

If you want to truly function as a team, to really live and breathe together, we believe there are five significant steps that you need to undertake in your startup.

These five steps are:

1) The Basic Needs of the Individual
2) Autonomy
3) Individual Mastery
4) The Purpose of the Purpose
5) Guarding the Gate

Principle Three is all about building on what you've gained. It's about taking the valuable steps in Principle Two, establishing your vision, values and alignment and using them to get the core of the people on your team, or the people you are selecting for your team. Following through the five steps of Principle Two will allow you to drill down deeper with your team, to find meaningful connections and create lasting alignment as a team and as individuals.

STEP ONE: THE INDIVIDUALS BASIC NEEDS

"Our mission statement about treating people with respect and dignity is not just words but a creed we live by every day. You can't expect your employees to exceed the expectations of your customers if you don't exceed the employees' expectations of management."

— Howard Schultz

The human brain doesn't come with an off switch. We've all spent many nights tossing and turning in bed, we'll almost be asleep and then for some reason convince ourselves that we left the oven on. We know we didn't, but in that moment we are absolutely certain we did. As incredible as our brains can be, they can be a little difficult at times. For entrepreneurs the random thoughts that keep you up seem to multiply whenever you try to rest. This makes for one resounding fact: People worry.

When you allow people the opportunity to let their mind carry and distract them, it will. It's a guarantee that there is something outside of work that will cause people to worry. This doesn't mean that you should try to make your employees conform to a belief or limit them in what they do and do not have access to. Instead, it is more beneficial to nurture and support them. More often than not, restrictive workplaces create increased concern in an employee. As freedom becomes stifled people tend to build resentment, which in turn creates more panic and worry. Especially in industries as volatile as startups, the key to a focused and aligned employee is to alleviate their outside worries as best you can.

There are always outside circumstances to worry about, but a lot of those circumstances stem from what an employee does or does not receive from their workplace. If you ensure that the basic needs of an individual are looked after and are not a worry to your team, then you permit them to be present in the workplace. Almost regardless of their situation, this will be an ongoing struggle for every startup. Money is often tight and paying lucrative salaries is generally out of the question. That being said, money is not always the actual problem despite statements saying otherwise. Employees expect a certain standard of living and without meeting that in some way, there is a gap in their perceptions and realities. Benefits tend to be just that, benefits, and while they can be expensive to the startup, the cost of providing the right team with them should be outweighed by their increased productivity.

What is essential to laying this foundation of support is providing service to your team. Their needs will always be far ranging and unique to each individual, so it's important to find out the services that are most needed and strive to provide those. Running a successful team doesn't mean being everything to everyone, but it does mean limiting the core worries and helping with the outliers as necessary.
There is a fine line to walk here as an organization. You want to

be accommodating to your employees and find out what their greatest needs are, yet at the same time you don't want that to cripple the organization. Both have to be in service to the other and while that means walking a narrow balance beam, it's important to the survival of the organization. An iterative process works best, over time bringing in different pieces of the puzzle to begin forming a robust solution. This alleviates outside worries slowly and builds loyalty with your team throughout the process. This may mean ensuring that healthcare, psychological and family needs are supported, along with encouraging vacation time to be taken for alignment or that wage levels are competitive. Find out the significant and key issues that are facing your employees and aim to meet those that keep recurring. If the majority of your team doesn't drive and takes public transit, create programs to ease the cost burden. Find solutions that recognize the pain points of your employees and meet them.

Teams are critical in startups. There is no other way around it. If your team, however, is spending their time worrying about money, prescriptions, child care and not working, your startup will suffer. Teams are critical and if they aren't functioning they become a massive detriment. The important item to recognize about your team is that they are human. They are never on their game 100% of the time, 24 hours a day, 7 days a week. It's not possible and it's unreasonable to expect it. What binds good teams together and builds startups is the elimination of outside sources of conflict that detract from the effort people are able to expend. After all, we'll have enough internal conflict to worry about without the difficulties outside of work.

We all want to adhere to the logic of leaving your personal life at home, but in reality this is an unrealistic expectation. There is never ending talk of finding a work/life balance, but the problem is that there is no such thing, at least not immediately after founding a startup. Even years after a company is up and running there is still no guarantee of ever finding a proper work/life balance. Team are vastly important and if they can't focus then they can't work, but if you take care of the team you have assembled and provide them with what they need to allow their mind to focus, the work they produce will be amazing.

The Principle from there becomes simple: take care of the team and the team (including you) will take care of the startup. When you get the right employees, and those employees are able to focus and work, they are able to accomplish the lofty goals your startup has set out to reach. When people worry, or have the time and space to fret, their performance dwindles and their stress level increases, whereas engaged employees tend to have the opposite reaction.

STEP TWO: AUTONOMY

"Management isn't about walking around and seeing if people are in their offices, it's about creating conditions for people to do their best work."

— Jeff Gunther

The second step of building a successful team for your startup is providing autonomy for the individual. In general, people require a certain level of direction and self-governance in order for them to feel that their contributions are worthwhile in the workplace. Even at the best of times it is a tricky slope to find yourself on. We all want to implicitly trust that our employees are using their time wisely, we do after all pay them for it, while at the same time wanting them to have the freedom to grow professionally in their own ways. If you're hiring the right people, they will work towards and respect the startup's goals and vision, but in order to do that owners have to place trust in an employee's instincts and abilities, allow them to fail, make mistakes and recover. Autonomous time, when productive, can be an amazing driving force for the success of a startup. As a general rule of thumb, we put into practice that about 20% of an individual's time should be of an autonomous nature.

Autonomous behaviours allow individuals to explore the freedom they are given in the workplace. As a result of this freedom they are able to explore their own self-worth, which is measured by their contributions. Team members already have the alignment that allows them to know exactly where they fit into the team and what affect their contributions have. In the free time team members are given they are left to their own devices to manage the projects they are currently working on, which allows them to measure what they feel to be the most important of their tasks or the most worthy of their time.

It is in this time that an employee will generally begin to work on projects that further the goals of the startup itself. These will sometimes be tiny bolt on solutions that make products flow faster or ways to streamline services offered. As employees continue to work on autonomous projects they become further engrained in the vision of the startup and continually associate their goals with the alignment of the startup. The autonomous time of an employee will generally be a reflection of the alignment they have created with their PEP.

As your team members begin to manage their time around projects they begin to take on greater amounts of responsibility for not only these projects, but in the workplace as a whole. By providing a certain degree of autonomy to individual team members you are encouraging their best work to be put forth. By attaching their names to projects or work that is purely created under their own time management, team members begin to prove not only their self-worth, but what they feel they are worth to the startup as a whole. This allows the strongest employee personality traits to become visible within these projects, helping both the individual and the team to determine where their best work can be done. Just because an employee was hired for a specific role, does not mean this is their best fit, unless the job is very specific in its requirements. Chances are that employees at a startup are going to be wearing as many hats as possible and their autonomous work roles allow them to find the hats that fit best.

Autonomy, however, can be a double edged sword. If the startup you're building is going to have autonomous time allocated to team members, then you must find employees who are comfortable and capable with this situation. Not all potential team members will thrive in an environment where they are left to their own devices and decreased direction.

You'll recognize them very quickly. They will be the types that either do not take any ownership and leadership surrounding their activities or those that simply waste their time. In these situations there needs to be stringent rules placed around autonomous work, which may seem contradictory. Nonetheless, guidelines around autonomy and the expectations of independent work time are necessary items in the early stages of a company to ensure it does not become a problem in the long run. These types of employees may shirk away from the responsibility of their own management and reject the want to have solely their name attached to a project.

Sustainable Startups need to embrace the often contradictory nature of guidelines around independent work times to truly excel, but both sides need to respect the borders and guidelines of the job's nature. When there is clarity and alignment within a startup amongst team members and founders, there also needs to be trust placed in the employees ability to contribute at all times. One of the most important aspects of autonomous work time is the founder's ability to trust the survival and well-being of their Sustainable Startup to their employees. Right or wrong, success or fail, the willingness to try must be present.

STEP THREE: INDIVIDUAL MASTERY

"People with a high level of personal mastery are able to consistently realize the results that matter most deeply to them - - in effect, they approach their life as an artist would approach a work of art. They do that by becoming committed to their own lifelong learning."

— Peter Senge

People want to be recognized, especially when they are part of a team. We fight our entire lives to carefully construct our identity, who we are and how we are perceived by those around us. We want recognition for our successes and approval when we rise from the ashes of our failures. There seems to always be a desire to make sure our name is etched somewhere in the history books. This, when left unchecked, can very easily come at the expense of the functionality of a team and while the growth of the individual should be important to the organization, if it comes at the expense of the success of the team then there are serious issues that need to be addressed.

When individuals become members of a team, this is a want that needs to be addressed before the desire for recognition gets in the way of the team's production. It is mandatory that individuals are able to recognize not only where their strengths lie, but the strengths of those around them as well. Team sports, much like startups, are not about a group of people supporting one superstar, rather it's a team of great individuals working together towards a common goal. When this vision gets lost in translation, the success of the team begins to waver.

Bringing together a team that understands their unique talents is a very powerful tool for a successful startup. The key to utilizing this is to make sure your team members are able to realize where their strengths lie and how they best contribute.

There are two questions that we like to ask in determining these talents:

1) How do I contribute to the team?
2) What do I contribute to the team?

It is important to have each member of the team answer these questions, to really focus and think them through before arriving at their answers. Review the questions and answers with each team member individually before and after the project, as well as conducting a 360 peer review of each member as a team to help gain the perspective of others on where individual strengths lie. Doing this type of review allows the individual to see where their perceptions line up with those of the team, allowing their realities to come closer together.

This will help your team members to recognize where their strengths and unique talents lie, however this is just the first step. Mastery of these talents does not just grow from recognition and expression alone. Mastery requires work and work in service to the company. Sustainable startups require teams that not only function together, but grow together.

How we like to best accomplish this is by having individuals teach, train and explain their contributions to their fellow team members. Look for opportunities for them to do this through their blog, lunch & learns, or by giving a formal training session. When you give people the opportunity to recognize and develop their unique contributions you create a team that uses these strengths to benefit the group and startup and not just fly solo purely wanting recognition for their own work.

STEP FOUR: THE PURPOSE OF THE PURPOSE

"Many men go fishing all of their lives without knowing it is not fish they are after."

— Henry David Thoreau

An area that is often overlooked when building a team is the one that determines the purpose of the individual and how that works in conjunction with the team. Of course in order for this to be in alignment and effective, the purpose of the team has to be clear, concise and well communicated to all members. Assuming your team is clear on its Why you can then move forward and sit down one on one with your team members to determine their individual Why.

The first step to doing this is to have each member of your team answer the following question: Why do I exist on this team? It's a question that not only plagues people from a professional perspective, but in our personal lives as well. While it may be impossible to provide a complete answer, giving scope and definition to an employee's end goal helps shape their productivity.

Once this question is answered the next step is what we like to call "The Five Why's." Much the same way that children will continually probe for answers by asking "Why?" we do much the same. Ask the individual "Why?" five times and by the end of the fifth answer you will have their true purpose on the team. You may find that what the individual believes their purpose on the team is differs greatly than where you believe their purpose lies. What is critical for alignment on your teams, however, is to ensure that you have selected the right people for it. The unfortunate part of business that occurs when dealing with purposes is the realization that the role is generally more important that the individual. At the end of the day that startup being pushed forward serves a greater purpose than the individual tasks of an employee. If they aren't providing a benefit and tasks are being shaped to meet their skill set then the startup isn't taking steps forward. Be prepared for a significant amount of pushback while walking through this exercise as it takes a lot of work and will fundamentally challenge an individual's view of their purpose.

What tends to happen is people can get defensive when they believe their usefulness is being questioned. No matter how prepared someone is, there is always a chance that they will be unable to separate criticism from an attack. As a result you may find that you have more work in front of you to place people on the proper teams or to find people that are the right fit for your organization. Nonetheless, it is more worthwhile to put the extra effort into assembling the correct team than letting a project fail because your startup has the wrong group of people for the job.

The second step in this process is to whittle the purpose you determined through asking "The Five Why's" down to a maximum of ten words. Work with your team members individually to determine if this is the most effective way that their Why can be explained and the significance that it holds for them.

In doing this exercise, you have helped to create the template for how your team members are going to contribute effectively to the team, while at the same time giving them a sense of purpose and self-worth.

STEP FIVE: GUARDING THE GATE

"To write down, frame, and publish your corporate values is all about self-deceit and ego. It is almost certainly bullshit."

— Barry J. Gibbons

Startups are not about the idea, they're about the people. It gets said a lot, but it is always worth repeating. Gathering a team of people to work at your startup is one thing, but gathering the right people will be an ongoing project.

The processes that have been laid out with the previous four steps of Principle 2 are designed to help you determine where your people fit best on your team. In doing these exercises you're always helping to determine if you have gathered the right people, as well as creating alignment for you personally and your team as a whole. If you have talented individuals who may be stand-outs in their respective fields, but those areas aren't relevant to your company, then you aren't doing your company and your team members any justice. Sustainable startups are about finding the right people for the right jobs and who are passionate about creating.

It is through these steps that you're creating corporate culture, the values and standards by which you operate. That being said, this process isn't a simple one off thing, it isn't over and done with by completing the exercises and steps that we've laid alone.

1) Stick to Your Processes – The 7 Principles.
We've just reached the end of Principle 3, so we have 4 more to go, however, as we continue toward the end of these Principles you will have a series of exercises you can implement on a continued basis to help protect your culture. The 7 Principles are designed for use within companies to help create Sustainable Startups. This is only done by understanding these Principles are not a onetime fix-all, but must be implemented in such a way that they become embedded into the culture you are protecting. We use repetition to cement habits into our daily life and the sentiment is no different for building a startup. The more focus we as entrepreneurs place on finding and filtering our team members, the more success we will have in building sustainable teams.

2) The "Yeah, But" Rule.
Protect yourself against excuses. People are prone to mistakes, the saying is "to err is human" for a reason, but excuses are costly. Whenever you find yourself, team members or other leaders in your organization starting a sentence with "Yeah, but..." you know there is trouble brewing behind the curtains. Startups, no matter the field, require their employees and teams to be wearing multiple hats at all times, so when people begin to let excuses slide it tends to have a domino effect across all the areas that they dip their feet into.

Failure is important in startups because it provides a learning experience and a pivot point. If teams or individuals shirk away from the responsibility and opportunity of a failure and begin making excuses, it can be toxic to the sustainability of the startup itself. Find the right area for team members to excel at or let them go. Shuffle them around or shuffle them out the door, either way you are not doing your team or your startup any favours by making excuses for employees that cannot execute fundamental tasks. Most importantly, you aren't doing that employee any favours by keeping them around. Employees inherently know whether they are willing to say anything or just let it slide.

3) Fail Fast.

This is a rule we live by. There is no greater way to learn than to fail fast and severely, but learning from shortcomings is impossible if you are unwilling to fail. When a project or team member is not working and not functioning in the team, you are hamstringing yourself by "giving them time to find their rhythm." We're not advocating getting rid of team members immediately if they do not pick up on the processes and roles, but instead to understand where the line is and that cuts need to be made when the line is crossed. In large corporations there tends to be a feeling that you are just another employee or that you get lost in the day to day shuffle. Startups are entirely different and generally speaking there is nowhere to hide. One of the biggest keys to a successful sustainable startup is to take ownership on both your successes and your failures. Employees, teams and companies learn just as much from their failures as they do from their triumphs.

Making sure you have the right people on your team is a continuous cycle. Guarding the gate becomes a process of filtering new entrants to make sure they fit in the parameters of your team structures, as well as protecting your current team. This isn't to say corporate culture cannot evolve and grow with new team members, but that it should be carefully guarded to help preserve the essence of the culture you and your team have created.

PRINCIPLE SUMMARY

The strength of Principle Three lies in creating the right team for your culture and startup. All ventures are inevitably going to be different, requiring different types of people in various roles at certain times. What all startups need, however, are people that work within and empower their corporate culture.

The five steps of this Principle build off of what we believe are the table stakes of team building. In Principle Two we outline them as the fundamental basics of building a team and in Principle Three we define what the fundamentals are in building the right team.

To successfully build your Sustainable Startup you need to understand the basic needs of the individuals that make up your team. Providing for your employees helps to keep them focused on their work and the success of the startup. The more minds are able to wander and worry about distractions the less focused they will be on the startup.

This is not to say that you should try to restrain employees from having time to think, rather that if you can take care of their basic needs you will increase their productivity.

Give your team members autonomous time to work on projects and allow them to accept responsibility for tasks they otherwise wouldn't. By placing responsibility in their hands you are helping to further their personal and professional growth. Addressing the strengths of your team members and supporting projects they can independently work on will not only strengthen the individual mastery they have of their skills, but provide purpose to their position as well.

Equally as important as building and strengthening your team
is preserving your team. Corporate culture is an ongoing process and a soft concept that is put at risk with every new hire
and fire that a startup goes through. In this respect, guarding
the gate of your corporate culture becomes an integral part of
the hiring process. Having an employee that is competent in
their position is important, but having one that contributes to
and evolves corporate culture is another. As always, every new
team members has an impact on the existing team, whether it
is good or bad. They shift and alter dynamics, which becomes a
check-in process with existing employees. Do they understand
why there was a new hire or why people were fired? Lack of
communication on small teams can very quickly lead to dis-
sension in the ranks of the existing team.

PRINCIPLE FOUR:
THE THREE REALITIES OF A STARTUP

"I reject your reality and substitute it with my own."

— Adam Savage

There isn't one definitive management alignment technique. In fact, there are many that border from cold, distanced and overly professional all the way up the ladder to hands on and excessively touchy feely. There is a fine line that works for each company and the reality of a startup always boil down to perception. Individuals react differently to various techniques and that's what makes them individuals, yet all these techniques are put in place to create alignment and a focused outcome. The unfortunate part of all alignment strategies is that while some may work well for a team, they may not be overly effective for the individuals within the team. We have found that alignment is fostered and grown in environments that recognize the realities of the individuals and not broad stroke techniques.

All alignment methodology, in theory, is only as good as the groups understanding of it. In order to create this understanding you need to do what your sales people advocate: going to where

your audience is. There is no overarching style that will create
alignment, but there are levels of understanding that create the
foundation of alignment within your corporate culture.

To develop this understanding we like to look at the three realities of alignment.

1) My Reality
2) Your Reality
3) Everything out of our control

These realities are based not only on our own experiences,
but our own unique biases that we place on these situations.
People are individuals, we all process information, emotions
and experiences differently, and due to this we will each have
our own distinct realities. Beyond that, we interpret information
on different levels than others, so while we can often relate to
a perspective, or have a shared understanding of a situation,
there are always nuances that define individual perceptions.

A large portion of managers, and the old style of business itself,
believe that alignment is top down. It's all about getting your
team to do what you want them to do for the reasons that you
want it done. In doing so, they create an environment where
goals are dangled in front of them and kept just out of reach.
This technique is effective when a company is developing a
workforce that is focused on achieving a manager's goal, but
not a team that is focused on developing and defining ideas.
This type of culture and alignment requires buy in from the
entire team and understanding from management.

This style of management in the 2.0 world doesn't fit and it
isn't sustainable. Rigid top-down hierarchies just don't function

anymore, at least not in typical startup situations. It's simply no longer the reality and for management to work there has to be a foundation of understanding created from the bottom up.

STEP ONE: MY REALITY

"Reality is merely an illusion, albeit a very persistent one."

— Albert Einstein

Understanding your reality will always come down to understanding what you want and how you want to get it. These are the views and biases that determine how we see the world and how we interpret events. While these views aren't the truth for everyone, they become the truth for you. The important part of the three realities that exist is to not get caught in any one, but to understand that all three exist simultaneously. This type of reality perspective is based on your rationalization of events.

When you catch yourself saying "yeah, but..." or "if only..." followed by an explanation, you are living in your reality. If you find yourself using an excuse to justify an action you've undertaken, then chances are you've become trapped in a very deep-seated rationalization.

As you try to rationalize your thoughts and actions you blind yourself to the realities of others. Allowing yourself to sink into your own reality creates a rift between you and your team members, which can be difficult to rectify if left unchecked.

Understanding the bias and views that exist within your reality allows you to take a step back to understand your rationalizations and in turn view more clearly the realities of others. We also place our own bias on situations we find ourselves in, it's human nature. As individuals we favour our own standing and positioning above others and more often than not we find our views of others opinions skewing against our own outlook. It's a hard road to get to an unbiased standpoint, but not one that is impossible.

While there is no proven method for instantly resolving the problems that arise from being in one's reality, there are some questions to ask yourself that do help the process. Again, they don't provide an immediate work around. More often than not there is a significant amount of conscientious effort that is required to keep you from slipping back into your viewpoints.

1) How do I see the current situation?
Ask yourself this question first and allow all your biases to flow through. While the question may not be answerable immediately, you will be able to see where you believe the problems or conflicts are coming from. It takes a lot to look at your situation and put into words exactly where you view yourself. Often times putting those thoughts and views regarding a situation into writing, while difficult, helps to articulate some of the areas our own thinking may vary from slightly.

2) What part of the situation frustrates me?
By answering this question you are able to examine not only what it is that frustrates you, but how it frustrates you as well. Recognizing where the distress is located in the conflict means you can identify where your biases are strongest. When dealing with situations we don't necessarily agree with, or that we find uncomfortable, it's a natural tendency to go on the defensive. More often than not this isn't overly conducive to projects getting completed or teams functioning together. When a project

fails, or looks to be stalling, it can seem like the entire thing is where frustration is stemming from. Taking a deeper look tends to reveal all the smaller intricate bits of the project that are building up and being able to see the small tension points apart from the whole is the first big step to remedying the situation.

3) What were my expectations of myself and how did I meet them?

In each situation we encounter every day of our lives, we place expectations on ourselves and others. These expectations, in turn, shape our view of a circumstance. By enabling yourself to see your successes and failures in a situation, or even how the expectations you placed on yourself were unreasonable, you are beginning to take yourself out of your individual reality.

4) What were my expectations of others and how did they meet them?

Seeing your own biases in a situation means examining the expectations you placed on others and what you expected them to deliver. By giving yourself the ability to see where expectations are in the situation and what the reality of the situation allows, you are once again giving yourself the ability to see and understand your biases.

5) How do I see the current situation?

Now that you have delved deeper into your understanding of the conflict and given yourself the ability to see where your biases were and how they affected your expectations, ask yourself this question again. This time use some of the realizations you've experienced throughout the previous questions to shape your understanding of the situations, free from your original rationalizations.

STEP TWO: YOUR REALITY

"There are no facts, only interpretations."

— Friedrich Nietzsche

The idea behind understanding Your Reality (as in someone else's) is to take a personal responsibility in finding their truth. Where Step One focuses on discovering your own truth and reality, Step Two is about discovering where the reality of others begins. Hearing another individual's interpretation of events can be exceedingly difficult. To start we almost always enforce our own biases upon whatever information we are being told. We may hear what they are saying to us, but as individuals we tend to take that information and put it against an overlay of what we already believe about the situation itself.

This is often done and best accomplished by placing yourself in a position of vulnerability and trust. Without truly understanding what biases you place on a situation, it's impossible to examine how another person interprets it. Situational awareness isn't a perfect solution, as it's impossible to take out all preconceived notions, but if you make yourself aware of where you stand you'll be better able to recognize when those judgements are getting in the way. Having already understood where and why your reality exists, placing yourself in this position helps to understand the reasoning and dissatisfaction of others.

To help others, pass along your answers to the Five Questions in Step One and ask the other members of the team to answer the same Five Questions below. Sharing your answers will help to share your level of commitment to solving the problems at hand. Having another team member see that you are willing to place yourself in a position of vulnerability in relation to a conflict can ease some of the upfront nervousness and anxiety that is often mingled in with conflicts.

While the questions are being answered by other team members, it's important to remember that realities, no matter how aligned, will always be different. Any of the realities presented will simply be interpretations of events and this is possibly the most difficult aspect to understand. No matter what happens, even if there is a clear right and wrong in the situation, people will have their own views and judgements. Not everything will be in black or white and when people become involved, more often than not situations tendto fall into the gray area.

1) How do I see the current situation?
Ask yourself this question first and allow all your biases to seep through. While the question may not be answerable immediately, you will be able to see where you believe the problems or conflicts are coming from.

2) What part of the situation frustrates me?
By answering this question you are able to examine not only what it is that frustrates you, but how it frustrates you as well. Recognizing where the distress is located in the conflict means you can identify where your biases are strongest.

3) What were my expectations of myself and how did I meet them?
We place expectations on ourselves and others in each situation we encounter every day of our lives. These expectations, in turn, shape our view of a situation. By enabling yourself to see your successes and failures in a situation, or even how the expectations you placed on yourself were unreasonable, you are beginning to take yourself out of your reality.

4) What were my expectations of others and how did they meet them?

Seeing your own biases in a situation means examining the expectations you placed on others and what you expected them to deliver. By giving yourself the ability to see where expectations are in the situation and what the reality of the situation allows, you once again give yourself the ability to see and understand your biases.

5) How do I see the current situation?

Now that you have delved deeper into your understanding of the conflict and given yourself the ability to see where your biases were and how they affected your expectations, ask yourself this question again. This time use some of the realizations you've experienced throughout the previous questions to shape your understanding of the situations, free from your original rationalizations.

STEP THREE: EVERYTHING OUT OF OUR CONTROL

"Are you really sure that a floor can't also be a ceiling?"

— M.C. Escher

The third reality of a Sustainable Startup is one of common ground. After identifying the expectations you placed on a situation in your reality and then the expectations of others when trapped in theirs, you are able to find where the misalignment in expectations and reality are.

Each reality seems right for those experiencing them. Your thoughts, emotions and rationalizations are all correct for you as you see them and the same applies for others who are trapped within their own realities. For others, how they see the situation around them is true. Every emotion, every thought and expectation is their individual view of the situation. In that case, while there can be a right and wrong outcome, each person in their view is often operating in a manner that seems correct for them.

The purpose of the five questions found in each reality is to help accomplish two things. The first is to separate the emotion of your reality, or others realities, from the expectations placed on yourself and others in the situation. People are very situational beings. When we see a scene begin to unfold we start to search for solutions in order to arrive at an endgame. As a result, we begin to speculate various outcomes based off of our own perceptions of a situation. Whether it is correct or not, this is now our expected outcome for a situation.

Secondly, these questions are used to create the foundations of alignment within your startup. If all of your goals and expectations are out of alignment then there are bigger questions and problems that need to be addressed in your startup. The three realities are about finding the roots of conflict and misaligned expectations within your company. In the end it must boil down to "What's right, not who's right," otherwise your startup is operating from a position of arrogance and ego. To do this however there are a few steps that we have found worked best for us.

1) List the goals of the situation:
With your team gathered, write down the goals you had been hoping to hit or the expectations you had in the situation. Once everything is out in the open you are able to do the following:

2) List what are the 3 most important things that need to get done to achieve our goals and who is responsible for each:
By narrowing the field of goals down to the three you deem to be the most important, you accomplish two things: First, you rid yourself of the excess goals and secondly, you create alignment within your team by saying, "these are the goals we're working towards, and we all decided their importance."

3) List how you know the 3 most important things are done:
Now that you've taken the time to examine what is and isn't in your control, and what goals are truly relevant to the situation, you have to measure them. The important step here is to measure these goals, and what you are doing to achieve them on a weekly basis, while being completely honest. We often want to exaggerate our progress, but it is important that team members push back when an answer is given to find the reasoning.

PRINCIPLE SUMMARY

Misalignment in any business can be crippling and nowhere is that more relevant than in startups. Working at a startup usually means long hours and changing directions on a very frequent basis. Pivots become a very real and regular aspect of business and something that needs to be made peace with as fast as possible. More important than pivots, however, are deliverables. The success of a startup is based around its ability to execute and deliver. When deadlines continually get extended, or team members are no longer delivering on their end, it can bring about some serious issues for your company. Working in this type of environment, while very rewarding, can create friction between team members easily, which is why it's imperative to have processes in place that allow you to resolve your conflicts. While there is no perfect system, with no guaranteed answers to resolve problems, the situations have a far greater chance of reaching resolution if each team member is able to remove themselves from their own personal biases and stigmas attached to the surrounding issue.

It's easy to get trapped in how you see the situation when dealing with conflicts. How it affects you, how you perceive the actions or inactions of others, these are the tell tale signs of being trapped in your reality. When you see yourself at the centre of the conflict and you are the key person interrupted by these problems, you as an individual are operating out of your own reality. Taking yourself out of the conflict means you can clearly see the three realities of a Sustainable Startup at play. Each member of the team exists in their own reality, within their own perceptions. Following the exercises laid out, the steps of the Principle Three can help to remove the biases that are placed around living in your own reality and allows the conflict to exist in a neutral area. By creating this neutral area, this reality of everything out of your control, you are able to tackle the true roots of the conflict and work toward a resolution.

PRINCIPLE FIVE:

PASSION IS THE NUMBER ONE CAUSE OF FAILURE IN STARTUPS

"What I fear and desire most in this world is passion. I fear it because it promises to be spontaneous, out of control, unnamed, beyond my reasonable self. I desire it because passion has color, like the landscape before me. It is not pale. It is not neutral. It reveals the backside of the heart."

— Derrick Jensen

Entrepreneurs, especially startup entrepreneurs, are notorious for their passion. There are few greater examples of people that believe so whole-heartedly in what they are doing than the startup entrepreneur. These are the people that live and breath their company every waking second of every day. They can give you an elevator pitch without hesitation and can transition between a deep dive explanation and a high level skim in a matter of seconds. Most business writing you'll read will probably tell you that this is good thing, that passion is the number one key to success in a startup. We propose that they are wrong in a big way. While some of the traits we link to passion are correct, the summation of its success is off base. We would even go so far as to say that passion is the number one reason for failure in startups.

Passion is an emotion built on attachment and ego. It's a great emotion to have and essential to a startup, but is something that needs to kept in check. Without passion your startup isn't going to go anywhere too fast, but with passion running uncontrolled through a startup you are just as likely to spend time spinning your tires in the mud. Uncontrolled passion is a sure a sign of an impending implosion. Startups that attach to their product or service with the knowledge that it is the right way risk everything based on a bias. This passionate belief that their way is the right or the only way is a surefire way to send a company spiralling downwards. This attachment and emotional trigger forms a bias around the **How** of an idea, or startup, not the **Why.**

What is really being talked about is tenacity. Tenacity is the relentless, dogged pursuit of your **Why.** It's not about who has the right way of getting something done, but instead focusing on what the right thing for your startup is. As was addressed in Principle Two, your idea isn't that important. Getting caught up in **How** you do something will only serve to hamstring your success, but truly understanding your **Why** will allow you to pursue that goal with relentless doggedness.

If you want to truly embrace your tenacity and keep your passion in check there are two steps we like to follow:

1) Clarity & Alignment
2) Measurement

STEP ONE: CLARITY AND ALIGNMENT

"Clarity affords focus." — Thomas Leonard

Keeping passion in perspective and egos in check is often like
watching a sheepdog round up a flock of sheep. It requires abso-
lute diligence at all times and the knowledge that sometimes,
a little bite isn't a bad thing, but is in fact necessary. Keeping
control is important, but when too much emphasis is placed
on control it can be just as limiting as letting emotion run wild.
Startups are geared towards finding the line and managing to
keep that delicate balance in tact.

Passion and tenacity can work together in a symbiotic rela-
tionship as one feeds the other and constantly pushes its
boundaries. Tenacity chasing passion is almost as dangerous as passion alone. Tenacity drives startups while unbridled
passion destroys them. Often it is passion that keeps an idea
driving forward, or pushes boundaries into new territories,
while tenacity helps to temper expectations and keep goals and
milestones on track. Keeping both in check requires two very
simple yet complex things: Clarity and Alignment.

Clarity:
Teams and individuals need to know why they are doing what
they're doing. Whether it's long term, short term or just daily

tasks, there needs to be a system in place that helps guide these actions. As we discussed earlier, this lack of understanding can evoke feelings such as a fear of mortality in an individual. For team members and founders there is very little difference. Everything breaks down to needing to know how and why you contribute and what your contribution adds to the overall growth of the startup. Clarity becomes about seeing how the actions of each team member affects the picture, both big and little. Without being able to imagine the picture at large, the end goal that each individual team member is contributing to evaporates and is replaced by a myriad of mundane tasks repeated daily. Much the same way that Principle One is designed to determine a company's **Why**, Step 1 helps to create the **Why, How** and **What** for each team member.

Why am I doing what I'm doing?

How am I going to get my "Why" done?

What is the day to day result of what I do?

Having your team members ask these questions of themselves will help them achieve clarity within their position and in their actions. If you are having a "passion" or ego problem with a team member, have them do this exercise and review it in conjunction with the **Why, How** and **What** or your **Why, How** and **What** to determine where you differ and how you can change for the better.

Alignment:
In Principle One, alignment is encouraged through the creation of Personal Elevator Pitch (PEP) and while the PEP is effective for determining an individual's role, an extra step is required to help keep the ego in check.

This extra step requires a lot of initial footwork to create a culture that allows for pushback from all employees. Constructive conflict in a startup is used to pushback against ideas, not to discredit and dissuade, but to get to the core of the idea itself.

Constructive conflict is a necessary measure to keep egos in check and passion in perspective in startups.

1) How is it currently done?
Gather your team or those having passion problems and sit down to discuss the situation. Write down How each member specifically accomplishes their PEP.

2) Is there a different way?
Have all members sit down and discuss other ways in which the How can be accomplished. This is a brainstorming session, so let every idea get put forward and discussed.

3) Vote it through.
After the brainstorming is done have each member of the team vote for their top three methods. Attach numbers to each idea: 3 for most valuable, 2 for second, 1 for least. After each member has voted add up the numbers to determine which is the agreed upon method of accomplishing How.

There is often a great deal of attachment to ideas when they are presented or suggested. People tend to emotionally invest themselves in solutions or suggestions they have put forward. The inverse of this is also true as team members will occasionally pass off their opinions in favour of supporting those of upper management. As a Founder, it is imperative that your opinion is the last to be expressed in order to not influence the opinions of others. This passion and attachment can become problematic when ideas are challenged. Creating situations of constructive conflict in which ideas are challenged removes the personal link between people and the ideas. There is always an attachment to an idea that is presented by an individual and however small it is, there is always a want for our ideas to be the best one. Removing this stigma is extremely difficult, but in order for brutally honest constructive conflict to occur the situation must be about what is right, not who is right.

If passion can be removed and the focus can be placed on what the idea represents, teams can effectively determine whether the idea is beneficial to your startup or not.

STEP TWO: MEASUREMENT

"The only man who behaved sensibly was my tailor; he took my measurement anew every time he saw me, while all the rest went on with their old measurements and expected them to fit me."

— George Bernard Shaw

Measurement is an extension of alignment. It is the next necessary step to keep passion in perspective and egos in check. It is often said that if something cannot be measured, then it isn't truly real and without measurement the clarity and alignment you have achieved through Step One will be ineffective, if useful at all. The only trick here is to be sure you're measuring the correct thing. Measuring vanity metrics, things that look good with no influence, can be a disaster for young startups. Often these metrics are used to hide facts or change a narrative to put a more positive spin on a situation. Positive is not always better as a lot of cycles and energy can be wasted on tracking and monitoring incorrect data. This is why measurement should always go hand in hand with alignment. One without the other is much the same as the blind leading the blind.

The ability to measure your How in a startup is effectively how you will gauge your successes, failures and findings. In this case, what you will be looking to measure is your What. In other words, what do you do and what will you be doing to accomplish your How.

In a business, finances and goals are generally tracked on a quarterly basis and we don't for a second suggest deviating from that. Quarterly reporting and tracking of goals allows for companies, managers and team members to understand what they are doing while at the same time seeing how it is important to the company. Taking the time to measure goals on ninety day cycles allows teams to compensate and alter their directions when they discover something isn't working or when new opportunities present themselves. Maneuverability is one of the most important aspects of a Sustainable Startup. The ability to see trends forming, understand the data as to why they've occurred and make adjustments on the fly is a tell tale sign of a Sustainable Startup.

Measurement, however, isn't just about reporting and gauging at the end of ninety days; it involves an incredible amount of diligence. To effectively measure yourself and others you need to know specifically what you will be working on, or towards, and be comfortable measuring your progress on a weekly basis. A method we have found to be effective for doing this is to complete the following process twice: once for setting the goals of the team and a second time to set the individual goals of each member to have them effectively work towards accomplishing the objectives set for the team.

1) Write it down.
As you should with all brainstorming sessions, write them down. Whether this is for setting team or individual goals, start writing. The easiest way to get ideas flowing, especially ideas that fall in line with the company goals, is to start writing and brainstorming.

By doing this, you are increasing your understanding of the direction the team is going and they are helping themselves as well. The important thing to remember is to always set a measurement guideline with every action.

If your action is to "Give Funding Presentations," there has to be a measurable quality to the action. Whether that is "Give Ten Funding Presentations," or "Give Ten Funding Presentations by May 1," if you are proactive in your measurements and meet on a weekly basis, these types of quantitative measurements will allow you to track and gauge your progress. By setting tactical goals with timeframes you are easily able to see which areas of the company bring in the most focus, what areas aren't being addressed and where problem or growth areas may be. Instead of just meeting at the end of ninety days to assess progress, it's important to schedule regular meetings to continue monitoring and checking in to see if the goals still reflect the aim and direction of the company.

2) Vote it through.
This isn't to say all the tasks and goals you've written down aren't important, but the vote it through process will allow you to determine what will be the top three goals you'll be working

toward over the next quarter. Chances are that each thing that was mentioned on your list of individual goals will come up and needs to be addressed during the quarter, but by putting it up and voting it through it eliminates extraneous goals and brings the team in to focus about what is most important.

This process of voting through, done either with the entire team or as individuals, helps to determine the focus of your goals. By selecting and voting as a team you are allowing the clarity and alignment practices you've done earlier to come to fruition.

For setting team goals, have each member of the team select which three things they believe to be the most important by attaching point values to them: 3 for most important, 2 for second most important and 1 for third most important. To determine the top three goals, add up all the votes and the goals with the three highest point scores become your objectives. For individuals, have them select their top three goals from all those listed. This allows individual team members to suggest and hopefully decide their goals for the next ninety days; goals that should fall in line with the goals set by the team for the team.

PRINCIPLE SUMMARY

Passion is a tricky thing to work with. At times it can be incredibly beneficial, it can uplift a team's spirits or rally employees to get behind an idea or cause. Passion can be both the savior and killer of a startup if it's left to its own devices, as passion can easily take hold of a situation and skew focus. While you may hear that passion is the key to success in a startup, it's important to note that in a Sustainable Startup it is also the number one cause of failure. Being passionate means walking a very thin line, and balancing between too much and too little, to the best of your ability every day to ensure the startup's survival.

Where passion doesn't allow for adaptability, tenacity allows startups to flow and grow, which are two of the most important aspects of a startup's success. Passion is a singular pursuit of an emotionally attached idea, while tenacity is the pursuit of a company's Why. Principle Five is about keeping your passions and tenacity in check and allowing your startup to remain focused on accomplishing the Why that supports it. Without the two working in conjunction, one will inevitably take control and squash the other. Blind passion is just as bad as constrictive control. This Principle is about creating focus on goals (90 day and 1 year), while adopting measurement cycles (weekly) to keep all members of the team accountable and working toward the same goals, while keeping passion and ego in check.

The processes of clarity, alignment and measurement work hand in hand, each requiring the other to function properly. Startups that begin with clarity and alignment, but have no measurement, will quickly lose focus and startups with metrics and analytical systems in place, but no goals to work towards, will end up spinning their tires in the mud.

PRINCIPLE SIX:

ACKNOWLEDGE MISTAKES AND DO WHAT IT TAKES

"Our greatest strength as a human race is our ability to acknowledge our differences, our greatest weakness is our failure to embrace them."

— Judith Henderson

Failure within a startup is a fairly frequent occurrence. In order for success to occur, failure must be something founders are familiar with. The important piece of that statement is not that failure happens often, rather that the opportunity to learn and grow exists more in startups than it does anywhere else. While seeing that side of the coin may not be the easiest accomplishment when things are looking extremely bleak, it's the ability to separate opportunity from failure that truly makes an entrepreneur stand out. Early stage companies and startups must grasp the ideology that being right is not the objective, but learning from their failures and mistakes is. Your end goal is always to create the right product to fit into the right market, but generally this requires a series of missteps along the way. For Sustainable Startups, the idea of picking yourself up off the ground, dusting off your knees and getting back into the game has never been more real and applicable.

Acknowledging mistakes in a startup is often a practice of stepping away from your ego, for both founders and employees. Where startups are, by nature, small groups of people working very closely together, a distorted sense of responsibility can easily develop. Much like in the Three Realities of the previous Principle, when the bias and ego is taken out of a situation, teams are able to address the real, underlying concerns. Team members may begin to assume credit for successes and place blame away from themselves when a project results in a failure.

Removing egos from a situation helps all those involved to see not only where they can improve, but how the team can be strengthened as well.

We've broken Principle Five down into Two Steps:
1) Acknowledge Mistakes
2) Do What It Takes

STEP ONE: ACKNOWLEDGING MISTAKES

"A man should never be ashamed to own that he is wrong, which is but saying in other words that he is wiser today than he was yesterday."

— Alexander Pope

Startups fail more than any other business. Not to say that they aren't or won't be successful in their own right, but that the opportunity for failure, regardless of scale, exists far more often than anywhere else. On the flip side of that coin, startups are a hotbed for advancement and innovation. Nowhere else is the pushing of boundaries more prevalent than within the four walls of a startup. These companies exist to find unique answers to problems, to find new solutions and new ways in areas of life that most people believe can't be further improved. In this scope of innovation the risks of failure, large or small, are significant. Within that area of possible and frequent failure, however, is tremendous space available for growth if startups are open to it.

Failing and learning from failures are two entirely different things and is what ultimately separates the successful businesses from those that succumb to failure. There is, however, a level of humility that is required to bridge the gap between learning and failing and acknowledging your mistakes, both personally and as an organization, is the first step. Creating a culture of accountability in your startup, which is part of the Sustainable Startup model, means taking responsibility for the mistakes that were made in projects and learning how to grow from them. After all, a failure is only a defeat if you learn nothing from it.

1) Being wrong is not wrong.

Overcoming the misconception that being wrong is bad requires a fair amount of humility within an organization. While people would clearly rather be right than wrong, making mistakes is an inevitable part of life and work. You will never get it right 100% of the time. In fact we'd wager you get it wrong more often than not. Taking the stance that mistakes are an opportunity to grow and learn as opposed to a time for blame and escaping accountability will help your organization grow.

2) Fail fast.

Accepting that being wrong and failure is okay are important steps for this Principle, but so is keeping your momentum going. When you fail there is an overwhelming urge to take time to lick your wounds and recover, to rest on your laurels and let the entirety of the situation sink in before moving forward again. What this does is lessen the impact that your failings have as it not only takes away the sting of the mistakes, but the energy to move forward as well. As children we were told to pick ourselves up off the ground and dust off our knees to try again, which is exactly the point of failing fast. Don't mull over your mistakes or failings, pick yourself up, find solutions, rectify your errors and attack it hard. Step Two of this Principle will outline some exercises that we recommend in order to do what it takes to turn your failures into successes.

STEP TWO: DO WHAT IT TAKES

"The price of greatness is responsibility." — Winston Churchill

Failing fast is the credo of the lean startup movement. The thought that when you fail individually, or as a startup, you need to pick yourself up as quickly as possible and move forward, which isn't what "failing fast" means at all. While it does imply that you shouldn't rest on your laurels and wait for the next revelation to come out of thin air, what it is really trying to tell you is that you should "fail smart." Picking yourself up and jumping headlong back into the fray isn't the right approach. You will simply make the same or different mistakes and uninformed decisions.

Take the time to understand why you failed, but use that time effectively. Be smart about it. Failing fast, or failing smart, means examining why the mistakes were made and how the problems can be fixed. To do this we suggest breaking your analysis of the situation down into five steps.

1) Look at what wasn't achieved or where the mistakes were made.

Take the time to examine exactly where the mistakes occurred and write them down. When you are looking into mistakes it is crucial to drill down as deep as possible and not just skim the surface. Deep problems can become systemic and bring down more than a single area of your startup. If you your goal was to get an initial Minimum Viable Product built from an existing product roadmap in 90 days and it doesn't follow through, you need to determine if it was simply a problem of deadlines or if there is something deeper at play. Was the product roadmap not complete? Were there pieces that were unnecessary? Was there a communications gap between development and prototyping? Without answering these questions the problem looks like it was simply a failure to execute, when in reality it could be significantly deeper and more widespread than that.

2) Prioritize your top three.

Chances are that when you begin to drill down into your problems, or the mistakes that were made, you'll begin to notice that there were either many issues or just offshoots of a single mistake. By prioritizing your top three mistakes you aren't saying that others identified aren't important and shouldn't be resolved, rather that the three you've selected should be solved first. If you come up with more than three, you need to keep track and address them with workarounds and solutions as soon as the three most pressing mistakes are solved. These problems, while they may seem minimal at the moment, can spread throughout the entire organization.

3) Why could these goals not be hit?

Sit down as a team and examine each of the three mistakes individually by asking "Why it could not be hit." Be careful not to place blame by asking "Why was this goal not hit," as you've already acknowledged mistakes and are now working to move forward.

4) What is the new goal?

Now that you've taken the time to understand exactly where the mistakes were and why they could not be hit, as a team it's time to decide what your next steps are. Using your learning from why your previous goals could not be hit will help you to develop strategies for creating and hitting new goals.

5) What needs to be done, by when, to achieve this goal, and by who?

Now that tasks have been created, responsibility needs to be assigned within the team. Part of acknowledging mistakes is accepting where responsibilities are going to lay. Take time as a team to structure timeframes and measurements to help accomplish the new goals you have set. One of the biggest problems that a startup faces is the sense of attachment that becomes engrained in employees and founders. In organizations, both large and small, delegation is frequently a problem, though at opposite sides of the spectrum.

Startups are almost entirely incapable of delegation. These are organizations where everyone must wear as many hats as possible to keep the company floating and growing. This is almost inevitable, but what comes along with it should be something that is monitored and addressed where necessary. When we start a project we want to see it come to fruition and these become our babies. While we may not have the best skills in place over and above another team member, when it is our project we're reluctant to relinquish the slightest bit of control. This mentality is beyond toxic to a startup environment. As a founder, if you don't have faith in your employees to handle a situation, then you've hired the wrong people.

PRINCIPLE SUMMARY

Principle Six focuses on responsibility. The mantra of "mistakes were made, but not by me," as talked about in the book of the same title by Carol Tavris and Elliot Aronson, is a detrimental mentality and harmful to a Sustainable Startup. Pushing responsibility onto others creates more problems than the initial root conflict, is bad for corporate culture and creates tension and unhappiness amongst team members.

Acknowledging mistakes is the first step towards assuming responsibility, both as individuals and a team, to rectify errors. Startups fail and make mistakes, that's the nature of the business no matter what "business" you're in. The success of startups and their ability to pivot, to bounce back from their failures, lies in their willingness to fail smart.

By acknowledging the mistakes made and doing what it takes to remedy the situation, Sustainable Startups embrace the fail smart mentality. This is the idea that mistakes and failures, while they may stem from a particular team or team member, are the responsibility of the entire startup. Each member is responsible for pivoting where it is necessary, learning from the mistake and moving forward with knowledge from their failures.

PRINCIPLE SEVEN:

GIVE AWAY WHAT YOU'VE LEARNED IN SUPPORT OF PROSPERITY

"In today's environment, hoarding knowledge ultimately erodes your power. If you know something very important, the way to get power is by actually sharing it."

— Joseph Badaracco

A startup is an organization that has created something great from a simple concept. You've taken your team and idea, approached it tenaciously while keeping your passions in perspective, and grown it into a Sustainable Startup with a team that is able to communicate and scale together. While being poised to grow and able to scale are important for any startup, giving away what you've learned is a priority for a Sustainable Startup.

The immediate concern that arises tends to be about trade secrets or competitive advantages you've created during your startup's run. There are certain things which will probably remain inside your business, after all Google doesn't readily display its algorithms to its competitors, however, sharing your k nowledge, tactics and strategies creates a community around your startups and feeds experience down through the entrepreneurial ecosystems. We believe there are five primary reasons that as a startup you should give away what you've learned in support of prosperity.

1) If you've created a successful, Sustainable Startup, creation is your first instinct, not hoarding.

The first instinct for creative individuals is to share their creations and continue to innovate. Artists don't produce their works and keep them to themselves just as writers don't write novels to then hide them away in safes. Their instinct is to share what they've accomplished and continue to create. Creation in a startup is no different, as many of the most prominent startups and entrepreneurs are those that have immersed themselves in the cycle of creation, completion, sharing and creation.

2) Hoarding is the same as admitting you can't do it again.

Giving away what you've learned and sharing your experiences means you can accept the challenge of starting again with an even playing field. By contributing your knowledge to the startup ecosystem you are proving to yourself that you are capable of repeating your successes.

3) You are not operating in secret.

Especially in the era of Web 2.0, very little is secret and even less remains that way for long. As we've mentioned in earlier Principles, there are no new ideas, simply different perspectives and to assume your project, or projects, are secret and unique is misguided.

4) Innovation always evens the playing field.
Innovation happens at such an incredible rate that any perceived advantages on one day can easily be erased the next. Share your ideas and techniques openly and be prepared not only to offer insight, but to be offered insight by other startup entrepreneurs.

5) Teaching creates new perspectives.
By sharing your knowledge and techniques you are accepting any questions that may come forward. Unwanted questioning can often create a defensive state of mind that closes the door to further creativity. Teaching what you know and accepting questions or criticisms allows you to see new perspectives and apply it in new ways.

Giving away what you've learned supports the startup industry, community and most importantly, your next venture.

PRINCIPLE SUMMARY

The final Principle of a Sustainable Startup works on the basis that the knowledge gained to craft a successful business is something that should be shared and never hoarded. Entrepreneurialism has a tendency to lean towards being an egotistical industry and while there is a sense of possession with the experiences you've gained, holding onto that knowledge is very similar to admitting to the rest of the industry that you can't repeat your success.

In Sustainable Startups the idea of sharing information is reciprocal. As knowledge, experience and expertise is shared amongst entrepreneurs, the door is open to insight to be received as well. This allows for processes to be built upon and expanded and for entrepreneurs to operate outside of a silo.

ACKNOWLEDGEMENTS:

Cassidy: You make me a better man everyday – Thank you for everything you are and everything we are becoming. I Love you, my soul loves you.

Carter, Harper, Wyatt: You are why I write and why I learn, so that others do not have to make the same mistakes I have made – I love you more than can ever be described.

Mom: For all the classes you drove me to, for the way you taught me to work and be focused, I can never repay you for what you have given me – I love you.

Family: Stan, Allan, Colleen, Walter, Lori, Brett, Courtney, Alex, Lorne, Christian, Nina, Ross, Colin, Hannah, Don, Myrna Thank you for your never ending support despite everything I have gone through. You have given me an amazing foundation upon which I have been able to grow – I love you all.

Partners: Rob, Erika, Paul R, Pat, Rod, Riaz, Mark, Craig, Kim, Rick, George, Thom, Raghu, Tom, Alistair, Vay, Cam S, Dale, Victor, Paula, Jamie, Arden, Aaron, Judy, Corrie, Paul B, Blair, Brad, Bob, to everyone else at BIG and those to numerous to mention who I have been lucky enough to work with in the past – thank you for what you have shown me and for what we have created together.

Jamie: I can't think of anybody better to be doing this with. Thank you.

– Cam

ACKNOWLEDGEMENTS   91

Thank you to Liz, without your support and devotion I couldn't be half the person I am today. Mom, Dad, Paul, Robb, Meg, Chelsea, Melinda, Emma, and Sutton, you all have shaped everything I am and helped me think in ways I had never thought possible. To all the friends and family I haven't mentioned, your support means the world to me, and I can never truly describe the impact you've had on me. Thank you to Shannon, Corrie and Steve for understanding "One more thing" will never, ever, mean one more thing, and lastly thank you to Cameron for the opportunity to be his partner and going on the journey of writing this book together.

-Jamie

TO THE TEAM AT BUSINESS INSTINCTS GROUP:

Your passion, dedication, and loyalty are a daily inspiration. Your crazy, unmatched creativity is what drives us forward and what will push us to unmatched heights. Without your collective leadership, candor, and powerful thinking we couldn't be where we are, we couldn't be who we are. Thank you for everything you do, everything you have done, and everything we will continue to do together.

-Cam and Jamie

ABOUT THE AUTHORS

CAMERON CHELL
CEO, Business Instincts Group

Cameron Chell has built several start-ups as well as being the Founder of Futurelink, the original cloud computing company. He is also the Co-Founder of UrtheCast, the first commercial video platform from space, Slyce, the visual purchasing engine and Cold Bore Technology, the Oil & Gas downhole communication platform.

JAMIE CLARKE
Senior Analyst, Business Instincts Group

Jamie Clarke works with entrepreneurs to produce relevant and remarkable content across multiple platforms. His articles have been picked up and shared by a variety of industry leading organizations. Jamie spends his time in the sales and marketing departments of small businesses and startups helping to drive user conversion and growth.

Made in the USA
Charleston, SC
27 July 2014